The Hidden Path

Exploring the Esoteric Traditions and Their Connections to Freemasonry

Elijah Abner

DEDICATION

This book is dedicated to the builders and safe keepers of the craft. May it bring light to your darkness, comfort to your troubled soul, and compassion to your weary heart while on your masonic journey.

CONTENTS

Know Thyself

Chapter 1 The Origins of Esotericism

An overview of the history and development of esoteric traditions, including their connections to ancient cultures and religions.

The history of esotericism can be traced back to the earliest civilizations, including the Sumerians, Babylonians, and Egyptians, who had elaborate systems of belief that included the use of esoteric practices and symbolism. These cultures often believed in the existence of hidden or secret knowledge that was only accessible to a select few.

In ancient Greece, the philosopher Pythagoras is credited with developing many of the esoteric practices that are still used today. Pythagoras and his followers believed in the existence of a divine order that could be understood through the use of mathematics and music. They also believed in the concept of reincarnation and the transmigration of the soul.

Esoteric traditions also played an important role in the development of Western philosophy and religion. In the Platonic tradition, the philosopher believed in the existence of a higher reality that could be accessed through the use of reason and contemplation. This higher reality was considered the realm of the Forms, which were abstract, eternal, and unchanging.

During the Hellenistic period, esotericism became more popular and widespread, with the emergence of new schools of thought and mystical movements. The Neoplatonists, for example, believed in the existence of a single, divine source from which all things emanate. They also believed in the importance of spiritual practices, such as contemplation and meditation, to achieve unity with the divine.

Esoteric traditions also played an important role in the development of religion in the ancient world. In Hinduism, for example, the concept of yoga involves the use of esoteric practices to achieve spiritual enlightenment. The word "yoga" means "union" or "joining" and refers to the union of the individual soul with the divine. The different schools of yoga teach various techniques, including physical postures, breath control, and meditation, to achieve this union.

In Buddhism, the use of meditation and visualization is a key aspect of esoteric practice. The Tantric tradition, which emerged in India during the 6th and 7th centuries, emphasized the use of complex visualizations and meditative practices to achieve spiritual transformation. The Tibetan Book of the Dead, which is a text used in Tibetan Buddhism, provides detailed instructions for the journey of the soul after death, and includes many esoteric practices to help guide the soul on its journey.

Esoteric traditions also played an important role in the development of Western religion. The Christian Gnostics, who emerged in the first few centuries AD, believed in the existence of hidden or secret knowledge that was necessary for salvation. They believed that this knowledge had been passed down from Jesus to his disciples, and that it was only accessible to a select few who had been initiated into the Gnostic mysteries.

The influence of esoteric traditions can also be seen in the development of modern science. Many of the early scientists, such as Isaac Newton and Johannes Kepler, were deeply interested in esoteric traditions and believed that the universe was governed by divine order. They saw their scientific work as a way to understand this order and to reveal the hidden mysteries of the universe.

Chapter 2 The Foundations of Freemasonry

An exploration of the origins and evolution of Freemasonry, including its roots in medieval stonemasonry and its development into a fraternal organization.

Freemasonry's evolution into a fraternal organization was not a sudden development. Rather, it was a gradual process that occurred over centuries. The stonemason guilds of the medieval period were highly organized, with a complex hierarchy and a set of values and principles that guided their work. The stonemasons were responsible for the construction of some of the most impressive buildings of their time, including cathedrals, castles, and bridges.

As the stonemason guilds began to decline in the 17th century, many of the values and principles that had guided them for centuries were in danger of being lost. However, a group of men who were interested in preserving these values and traditions formed the first lodges of Freemasonry. These lodges were based on the principles of brotherhood, charity, and personal growth, which had been central to the stonemason guilds.

Freemasonry quickly grew in popularity, and by the 18th century, it had spread throughout Europe and North America. The organization continued to evolve and develop, with new rituals, symbols, and teachings being added to the system of initiation. One of the key features of Freemasonry was the use of degrees or levels of membership, each with its own set of teachings and rituals.

The first degree of Freemasonry, known as the Entered Apprentice degree, was designed to convey the basic principles of the organization, including brotherhood, charity, and personal growth. The second degree, known as the Fellowcraft degree, delved deeper into the symbolism and teachings of Freemasonry, while the third degree, known as the Master Mason degree, was the highest level of membership and was reserved for those who had achieved a high level of understanding and proficiency in the teachings of the organization.

Freemasonry also played an important role in the development of the United States. Many of the founding fathers, including George Washington, Benjamin Franklin, and John Hancock, were Freemasons, and the organization had a significant influence on the ideas and values that shaped the new nation.

Despite its popularity and influence, Freemasonry has also been the subject of controversy and criticism. Some have accused the organization of being a secret society with ulterior motives, while others have criticized it for its exclusion of women and non-Christians.

In recent years, there has been a renewed interest in Freemasonry, with many young people seeking out lodges in search of community, personal growth, and esoteric knowledge. The organization continues to evolve and adapt to changing times, while still holding true to its core values of brotherhood, charity, and personal growth.

Chapter 3 The Secret Language of Symbols

An analysis of the role of symbolism in esoteric traditions, including how these symbols are used in Freemasonry.

Symbols are a fundamental aspect of esoteric traditions, with their use dating back to ancient times. These symbols are often used to represent complex ideas and concepts that cannot be easily expressed through language alone. In the context of esoteric traditions, symbols are used to communicate spiritual and mystical concepts to initiates, often conveying hidden meanings and deeper truths.

One of the most significant aspects of symbolism in esoteric traditions is its universality. Symbols are often used across cultures and throughout history, with similar symbols appearing in seemingly unrelated traditions. This suggests that these symbols may represent universal truths that transcend cultural and historical boundaries.

In the context of Freemasonry, symbolism plays a crucial role in the organization's rituals and teachings. Masonic symbolism is drawn from a wide range of sources, including ancient myths and legends, religious texts, and the tools and techniques of stonemasonry.

One of the most important symbols in Freemasonry is the square and compasses. This symbol represents the idea of measuring and building, and is used to convey the importance of morality, self-improvement, and personal growth. The square represents morality, while the compasses represent the limits of our actions and the need for self-control.

Another important symbol in Freemasonry is the all-seeing eye. This symbol represents the idea of divine providence and the omnipresence of God. It is often depicted within a triangle, which represents the three aspects of God: the Creator, the Redeemer, and the Sustainer.

The pillars of Jachin and Boaz are also significant symbols in Freemasonry. These pillars represent the idea of balance and stability, with Jachin representing strength and Boaz representing beauty. Together, they symbolize the importance of balancing strength and beauty in our lives.

Other symbols used in Freemasonry include the beehive, which represents industry and cooperation, and the trowel, which represents the spreading of brotherly love.

The use of symbols in Freemasonry serves several purposes. First, it helps to create a sense of unity and shared identity among members. Symbols can also be used to convey complex ideas and concepts in a way that is easily understood by initiates, helping to deepen their understanding of the organization's teachings. Additionally, symbols can serve as a mnemonic device, helping initiates to remember important lessons and teachings.

However, the use of symbols in Freemasonry has also been the subject of criticism and controversy. Some have accused the organization of using symbols to convey hidden messages and agendas, while others have criticized its exclusionary practices and alleged secrecy.

Despite these criticisms, the use of symbols in esoteric traditions and Freemasonry remains a powerful and influential aspect of these traditions. Symbols serve as a means of communication and education, helping initiates to deepen their understanding of complex ideas and concepts. They also help to create a sense of unity and shared identity among members, strengthening the bonds of brotherhood and community within the organization.

It is important to note that the interpretation of symbols in esoteric traditions and Freemasonry is often subjective and can vary widely depending on the individual and their personal experiences and beliefs. While some symbols may have a widely accepted meaning within the organization, others may be open to interpretation or have different meanings depending on the context in which they are used.

Furthermore, the use of symbols in Freemasonry is not limited to its rituals and teachings. Symbols can be found in Masonic art and architecture, as well as in the organization's regalia and insignia. These symbols serve as a reminder of the organization's values and principles, and are often used to communicate these values and principles to the wider world.

Overall, the use of symbols in esoteric traditions and Freemasonry is a complex and multifaceted aspect of these traditions. While symbols can be used to convey hidden meanings and deeper truths, they can also be used to create a sense of unity and shared identity among members. As such, symbols remain an important tool for communication and education within these traditions, and will continue to be a central aspect of their teachings for years to come.

In addition to their use in Freemasonry, symbols also play an important role in other esoteric traditions, such as Hermeticism, Kabbalah, and alchemy. These traditions use symbols to represent spiritual and mystical concepts, with each symbol carrying its own unique meaning and significance.

For example, in Hermeticism, the symbol of the caduceus is often used to represent the union of opposing forces, such as the masculine and feminine energies, or the spiritual and material realms. In Kabbalah, the Tree of Life is a complex symbol representing the ten sephiroth, or divine attributes, and their interconnectedness.

The use of symbols in esoteric traditions can also be seen in the practice of sigil magic. Sigils are unique symbols created for a specific purpose, such as manifesting a particular outcome or intention. The creation and use of sigils is often seen as a form of spiritual practice, with the symbols representing a connection between the individual and the divine.

Despite the importance of symbols in esoteric traditions, their use has also been the subject of criticism and controversy. Some argue that symbols can be used to manipulate and control individuals, while others suggest that they can be used to spread harmful or divisive ideologies.

However, it is important to recognize that symbols themselves are neutral, and their meaning and significance depend on the context in which they are used. It is up to individuals to critically evaluate the symbols they encounter and interpret them in a way that aligns with their own values and beliefs.

Chapter 4 The Four Elements and Their Significance

A discussion of the four classical elements (earth, air, fire, and water) and how they relate to esotericism and Freemasonry.

The four classical elements - earth, air, fire, and water - have been a central concept in esoteric traditions and Freemasonry for centuries. Each element carries its own unique symbolism and significance, and understanding their meaning can provide insight into the teachings and practices of these traditions.

Earth is often associated with stability, groundedness, and materiality. It represents the physical world and the tangible objects that exist within it. In esoteric traditions and Freemasonry, earth is often used to represent the body and the physical realm, and is associated with the element of stability and the divine feminine.

Air, on the other hand, is associated with movement, communication, and intellectualism. It represents the realm of ideas and abstract thought, and is often used to represent the mind and the mental realm. In esoteric traditions and Freemasonry, air is associated with the element of intellect and the divine masculine.

Fire is perhaps the most dynamic and transformative of the four elements. It represents passion, creativity, and destruction, and is often used to represent the transformative power of the divine. In esoteric traditions and Freemasonry, fire is associated with the element of transformation and the divine spark that exists within all things.

Water, meanwhile, is associated with emotions, intuition, and the subconscious. It represents the realm of the unknown and the unseen, and is often used to represent the spiritual realm. In esoteric traditions and Freemasonry, water is associated with the element of emotion and the divine feminine.

Together, the four elements form a symbolic representation of the world and the various aspects of existence. They represent the balance and interconnectedness of all things, and the importance of maintaining a sense of harmony and balance in one's life and spiritual practice.

In Freemasonry, the four elements are often used in rituals and teachings to represent various aspects of the organization and its teachings. For example, the four cardinal virtues - temperance, fortitude, prudence, and justice - are often associated with the four elements, with temperance representing water, fortitude representing earth, prudence representing air, and justice representing fire.

Overall, the four elements are a powerful symbol in esoteric traditions and Freemasonry, representing the balance and interconnectedness of all things. Understanding their significance can provide insight into the teachings and practices of these traditions, and serve as a reminder of the importance of maintaining balance and harmony in one's life and spiritual practice.

Furthermore, the four elements are also believed to correspond to different parts of the human body, as well as to different stages of personal growth and development. For example, earth is often associated with the feet and legs, and represents stability and groundedness in one's life. Air is associated with the lungs and represents mental clarity and the ability to communicate effectively. Fire is associated with the heart and represents passion and creativity, while water is associated with the reproductive organs and represents the power of intuition and emotions.

In addition to their physical and metaphorical associations, the four elements also play an important role in alchemical traditions, where they are often used to represent different stages of transformation and growth. For example, earth represents the beginning stages of transformation, where materiality and physicality dominate. Air represents the stage of intellectual development, where ideas and thoughts begin to take shape. Fire represents the stage of purification and transformation, where the old is burned away to make way for the new. Finally, water represents the stage of integration and completion, where the transformed individual is able to connect with the divine and achieve a sense of wholeness.

In Freemasonry, the four elements are often used in the creation of symbolic images and emblems, such as the Masonic tracing board. This board features a series of symbols and images arranged in a pattern that represents the journey of personal transformation and spiritual growth. The four elements are often featured prominently in these symbols, representing the different stages of transformation and growth that the initiate must pass through in order to achieve enlightenment.

Overall, the four elements are a powerful and versatile symbol that play an important role in esoteric traditions and Freemasonry. They represent the balance and interconnectedness of all things, and provide a framework for understanding personal growth and spiritual development. By exploring the significance of the four elements, we can gain a deeper understanding of the teachings and practices of these traditions, and find inspiration for our own personal journey of transformation and growth.

It is important to note that the four elements are not seen as static or fixed concepts, but rather as dynamic and ever-changing forces that are in a constant state of flux. They are constantly interacting with each other, and can be transformed and transmuted in various ways. This idea is reflected in the alchemical concept of transmutation, where base elements are transformed into gold through a process of purification and refinement.

In addition to their associations with the physical world and personal growth, the four elements also have a spiritual dimension. In many esoteric traditions, they are seen as representing different aspects of the divine, with earth representing the physical body, air representing the intellect, fire representing the spirit or soul, and water representing the emotions and intuition. This spiritual dimension of the elements is reflected in the symbolic language of Freemasonry, where they are used to represent the journey of the initiate towards spiritual enlightenment and the realization of their connection to the divine.

The use of the four elements in esoteric traditions and Freemasonry is a powerful reminder of the interconnectedness of all things, and the importance of balance and harmony in our lives. By understanding the significance of the elements, we can gain a deeper understanding of ourselves and the world around us, and find inspiration for our own journey of personal transformation and growth.

It is also worth noting that the four elements are not exclusive to esoteric traditions or Freemasonry, but are found in many different cultures and belief systems throughout history. In ancient Greece, for example, the four elements were seen as the building blocks of all matter, with each element having a corresponding god or goddess. In Hinduism, the four elements are associated with the four varnas or social classes, with earth representing the laboring class, water representing the artisan class, fire representing the warrior class, and air representing the priestly class.

Despite their widespread use and significance, the four elements are often overlooked or dismissed in modern society, which tends to place more emphasis on rationality and science. However, by reconnecting with these ancient symbols and concepts, we can tap into a deeper level of understanding and awareness, and gain insights into the mysteries of the universe and our place within it.

Chapter 5 The Tree of Life

An exploration of the Kabbalistic symbol of the Tree of Life and its significance in esoteric traditions and Freemasonry.

The Tree of Life is a complex and multifaceted symbol that has played a significant role in many esoteric traditions, including Kabbalah, Hermeticism, and Freemasonry. At its core, the Tree of Life is a diagram of the process of creation, representing the interconnecting paths between various aspects of the divine and the universe. This symbol has been used as a guide for spiritual growth and development, with each sephira representing a different aspect of God or the universe, and each path representing a different stage of the journey towards spiritual enlightenment.

In Kabbalah, the Tree of Life is viewed as a blueprint for the universe, representing the divine attributes and the process of creation. The ten sephiroth are arranged in three columns, with the left column representing feminine or receptive energy, the right column representing masculine or active energy, and the central column representing balance and harmony between the two. Each sephira represents a different aspect of the divine, such as wisdom, love, and power, and the paths between them represent the process of creation and the journey towards spiritual union with the divine.

In Hermeticism, the Tree of Life is seen as a symbolic representation of the psyche, with each sephira representing a different aspect of the human psyche, such as intellect, emotion, and intuition. The Tree of Life is viewed as a tool for personal transformation, helping the initiate to achieve self-realization and spiritual enlightenment. The Hermetic interpretation of the Tree of Life also emphasizes the importance of balance and harmony between the different aspects of the psyche, and the need to integrate the various parts of the self in order to achieve wholeness and unity.

In Freemasonry, the Tree of Life is used as a symbol of the moral and spiritual values that are central to the fraternity, such as brotherly love, truth, and charity. The Tree of Life is viewed as a guide for personal transformation and spiritual growth, helping the initiate to develop the virtues and values that are necessary for a fulfilling life. The Tree of Life is also seen as a representation of the journey of the initiate through the various degrees of Freemasonry, with each degree representing a different stage of the journey towards spiritual enlightenment.

The symbolism of the Tree of Life can also be found in many other esoteric traditions, including alchemy, astrology, and tarot. In alchemy, the Tree of Life is seen as a representation of the various stages of the alchemical process, with each sephira representing a different stage of transformation. In astrology, the Tree of Life is associated with the twelve zodiac signs, with each sephira representing a different planetary influence. In tarot, the Tree of Life is represented by the Major Arcana, with each card representing a different stage of the journey towards spiritual enlightenment.

The Tree of Life is a powerful symbol that can be experienced directly through meditation and contemplation. By visualizing the sephiroth and meditating on their symbolism, we can tap into the transformative power of the Tree of Life and bring its energy and wisdom into our daily lives. The Tree of Life is a powerful tool for personal transformation and spiritual growth, guiding the initiate towards self-realization and spiritual enlightenment.

The Tree of Life is not only a symbol but also a tool that can be used for self-discovery and personal growth. Its complex structure and deep symbolism offer a wealth of insights into the nature of reality and our place within it. By exploring the different sephiroth and their corresponding qualities, we can gain a deeper understanding of ourselves and the world around us.

One way to work with the Tree of Life is through meditation and visualization. By focusing on each sephira in turn and meditating on its qualities and symbolism, we can begin to cultivate those qualities within ourselves. For example, meditating on the sephira of Chesed (mercy) can help us develop compassion and empathy, while meditating on the sephira of Netzach (victory) can help us cultivate perseverance and determination.

The Tree of Life can also be used as a framework for understanding the relationships between different aspects of our lives. For example, the sephira of Malkuth (kingdom) represents the physical world and our material existence, while the sephira of Kether (crown) represents the spiritual realm and our connection to the divine. By understanding the relationships between these different aspects of our lives, we can work towards greater balance and harmony.

In Freemasonry, the Tree of Life is used as a symbol of the journey of the initiate through the various degrees of the fraternity. Each degree represents a different stage of the journey towards spiritual enlightenment, with the ultimate goal being the attainment of the highest degree of Master Mason. The symbolism of the Tree of Life is woven throughout the various rituals and teachings of Freemasonry, providing a powerful tool for personal transformation and spiritual growth.

Chapter 6 The Tarot

A study of the symbolism and history of the Tarot, including its connections to esotericism and its use in Freemasonry.

The Tarot is a deck of cards that has been used for divination, meditation, and personal growth for hundreds of years. Its rich symbolism and powerful imagery have captivated the imaginations of many, and its use has spread far beyond its origins in Europe.

The history of the Tarot is shrouded in mystery and controversy, with some scholars tracing its roots back to ancient Egypt or even Atlantis. However, most historians agree that the Tarot as we know it today originated in Renaissance Italy, where it was used as a game and a tool for divination.

The Tarot consists of 78 cards, divided into the Major Arcana (22 cards representing archetypal energies and universal themes) and the Minor Arcana (56 cards representing everyday experiences and situations). Each card has its own unique symbolism and meaning, and can be interpreted in a variety of ways depending on the context and the reader's intuition.

In esoteric traditions such as Kabbalah and Hermeticism, the Tarot is seen as a tool for spiritual growth and self-discovery. The cards are thought to represent the various aspects of the human psyche and the journey of the soul towards enlightenment. By working with the Tarot, practitioners can gain insight into their own inner world and the forces that shape their lives.

In Freemasonry, the Tarot is sometimes used as a teaching tool, with each card representing a different lesson or principle of the craft. For example, the card of the Fool may represent the concept of innocence and the journey of the initiate towards wisdom and understanding.

The use of the Tarot in Freemasonry is not without controversy, however. Some Masonic scholars argue that the Tarot is not a legitimate part of the Masonic tradition, and that its use in Masonic contexts is a modern invention.

Despite these debates, the Tarot remains a powerful tool for personal growth and spiritual exploration. Its rich symbolism and deep history offer a wealth of insights into the human experience and the mysteries of the universe. Whether used for divination, meditation, or self-discovery, the Tarot has the power to unlock hidden truths and illuminate the path towards enlightenment.

The Tarot has also been associated with various esoteric traditions, including the Western Mystery Tradition and the Hermetic Order of the Golden Dawn. These groups saw the Tarot as a powerful tool for unlocking the secrets of the universe and connecting with higher spiritual energies.

In the Golden Dawn, the Tarot was seen as a way to connect with the Qabalistic Sephiroth on the Tree of Life. Each card corresponded to a specific Sephirah and could be used to meditate on the energies and attributes associated with that Sephirah.

Similarly, in the Western Mystery Tradition, the Tarot was seen as a way to access the archetypal energies of the collective unconscious. By meditating on the symbols and imagery of the Tarot, practitioners could tap into these energies and gain insight into their own psyche and the forces that shape the world around them.

The use of the Tarot in esoteric traditions and Freemasonry is a testament to the enduring power and significance of this ancient tool. Whether seen as a game, a divination tool, or a spiritual guide, the Tarot continues to captivate and inspire people around the world. Its symbolism and imagery offer a window into the mysteries of the universe and the depths of the human soul, and its teachings have the power to transform and illuminate the path towards spiritual growth and self-discovery.

In Freemasonry, the Tarot has been associated with the concept of the Royal Arch. This is a degree in Freemasonry that involves the symbolic rebuilding of the Temple of Solomon and the discovery of lost secrets. The Tarot has been used as a tool for exploring the symbolism and meaning of this degree, with each card corresponding to a different aspect of the journey towards the Royal Arch.

One of the most significant ways in which the Tarot is used in Freemasonry is in the form of the Tarot Trumps. These are a series of 22 cards that represent the Major Arcana of the Tarot. Each card is associated with a different attribute or principle, such as strength, justice, and wisdom. The Tarot Trumps are often used in Freemasonry as a way to symbolically represent the journey towards spiritual enlightenment and the attainment of higher levels of consciousness.

Another way in which the Tarot is used in Freemasonry is through its connection to the concept of alchemy. Alchemy is a tradition that seeks to transform base metals into gold, but also encompasses the transformation of the self and the attainment of spiritual enlightenment. The Tarot has been associated with alchemy because of its use of symbols and imagery to represent these transformative processes.

Chapter 7 The Hermetic Tradition

An examination of the Hermetic philosophy and its influence on esotericism and Freemasonry.

The Hermetic Tradition is an ancient spiritual and philosophical system that has had a profound influence on esotericism and Freemasonry. It is a set of teachings and practices that are believed to have originated in ancient Egypt and were later developed in Hellenistic Greece. The Hermetic Tradition is named after Hermes Trismegistus, a mythical figure who was said to be the founder of the tradition and the author of its sacred texts.

The Hermetic Tradition is based on the belief that there is a fundamental unity and interconnectedness between all things in the universe. This unity is referred to as the One, and it is believed to be the source of all creation. According to Hermetic teachings, the universe is not simply a random collection of isolated objects and events, but a living, intelligent organism that is continually evolving and unfolding.

The Hermetic Tradition emphasizes the importance of spiritual growth and self-transformation as a means of achieving a deeper understanding of the universe and one's place in it. It teaches that by aligning oneself with the divine will and by cultivating virtues such as wisdom, compassion, and love, one can transcend the limitations of the material world and achieve a higher state of consciousness.

The teachings of the Hermetic Tradition are expressed through a series of sacred texts known as the Hermetica. These texts include the Corpus Hermeticum, a collection of fourteen treatises that are believed to have been written in the early centuries of the Common Era. The Hermetica also includes a number of other works, including the Asclepius and the Emerald Tablet.

The Hermetic Tradition has had a profound influence on esotericism and Freemasonry. Many of the concepts and practices of the Hermetic Tradition, such as the importance of spiritual growth and the use of symbolism and ritual, are central to Freemasonry. The Hermetic Tradition has also had a significant impact on the development of Western occultism and mysticism.

The Hermetic Tradition has been particularly influential in the development of alchemy, a spiritual and philosophical tradition that seeks to transform base metals into gold and to achieve spiritual enlightenment. The alchemical process is seen as a metaphor for the transformation of the human soul, and the Hermetic teachings on the nature of the universe and the importance of spiritual growth are central to the practice of alchemy.

The Hermetic Tradition has also been influential in the development of astrology, a system of divination that uses the positions of the planets and stars to interpret human events and characteristics. The Hermetic teachings on the interconnectedness of all things and the influence of celestial bodies on human life are central to the practice of astrology.

Chapter 8 The Mystery Religions

A discussion of the ancient mystery religions and their connections to esotericism, including their influence on Freemasonry.

The Mystery Religions were ancient religious practices that originated in the Mediterranean region during the Hellenistic and Roman eras. These religions were characterized by secret initiation rituals, which were intended to reveal the mysteries of the divine to the initiated. The Mystery Religions were a major influence on esoteric traditions, including Freemasonry.

One of the most significant Mystery Religions was the Eleusinian Mysteries, which were held in honor of Demeter and Persephone in the city of Eleusis in ancient Greece. The initiation ceremony was a week-long ritual that culminated in the revelation of a sacred object or event that was said to reveal the secret of eternal life. The Eleusinian Mysteries were celebrated for over a thousand years and were considered the most important religious event in the ancient Greek world.

The cult of Isis was another prominent Mystery Religion, which originated in ancient Egypt and spread throughout the Roman Empire. The cult of Isis was based on the worship of the goddess Isis, who was believed to have magical powers and the ability to bring the dead back to life. The initiation ceremony for the cult of Isis was a secret ritual that was only revealed to the initiated. The cult of Isis was particularly popular among women and was one of the few religions in the ancient world that allowed women to participate in its rituals.

The Orphic Mysteries were another ancient religious tradition that had a profound influence on esotericism. The Orphic Mysteries were based on the teachings of Orpheus, a legendary musician and poet who was believed to have the power to communicate with the gods. The Orphic Mysteries taught that the soul was immortal and that it could be liberated from the cycle of birth and death through knowledge and spiritual purification.

The influence of the Mystery Religions on esotericism can be seen in the symbolism and ritual practices of many esoteric traditions, including Freemasonry. Freemasonry is often referred to as a "speculative" craft, which means that it is not based on the practical craft of stonemasonry, but rather on the symbolic interpretation of stonemasonry. The use of initiation rituals, symbolic language, and secret knowledge is a direct reflection of the influence of the Mystery Religions on Freemasonry.

The Masonic initiation ceremony, for example, has been compared to the initiation rituals of the Eleusinian Mysteries. The candidate is blindfolded and led through a series of symbolic trials and challenges, which are intended to test his character and prepare him for the revelation of Masonic secrets. Similarly, the use of symbolic language and imagery in Masonic ritual is reminiscent of the symbolism used in the Mystery Religions.

Chapter 9 The Alchemical Tradition

An exploration of the history and significance of alchemy, including its connections to esotericism and its role in Freemasonry.

Alchemy is an ancient tradition that seeks to transform base metals into gold, and to attain spiritual enlightenment and immortality through the transmutation of the soul. While often dismissed as a primitive precursor to modern chemistry, alchemy is in fact a rich and complex tradition that has influenced many aspects of Western culture, including esotericism and Freemasonry.

The origins of alchemy can be traced back to ancient Egypt and Greece, where philosophers and priests sought to uncover the secrets of nature and the universe through the study of minerals, plants, and animals. These early alchemists believed that everything in the world was composed of the four classical elements (earth, air, fire, and water), and that by manipulating these elements, they could achieve their goals.

During the Middle Ages, alchemy spread throughout Europe, where it became associated with the Christian mystical tradition. Alchemists believed that the transformation of base metals into gold was not just a physical process, but a spiritual one as well, and that the same principles that governed the physical world also governed the spiritual world.

In the Renaissance, alchemy reached new heights of sophistication and complexity, with many alchemists seeking to create a universal elixir or philosopher's stone that would not only transmute base metals into gold, but also grant immortality and spiritual enlightenment to those who consumed it. The works of famous alchemists such as Paracelsus and John Dee, as well as the Rosicrucian movement, drew heavily on alchemical principles and symbolism.

The influence of alchemy on esotericism and Freemasonry can be seen in many of their symbols and rituals. The alchemical process of transmutation, with its emphasis on the purification and transformation of matter, is often seen as a metaphor for the spiritual transformation of the individual. The alchemical symbol of the ouroboros, a serpent eating its own tail, represents the cyclical nature of creation and the idea of the eternal return.

In Freemasonry, alchemy is often referred to as the "Royal Art," and is seen as a key component of the Masonic journey. The Masonic symbol of the square and compass, which represents the principles of harmony and balance, can be seen as a representation of the alchemical goal of transmuting base matter into something of higher value.

Overall, the alchemical tradition is an integral part of esotericism and Freemasonry, and continues to inspire and influence seekers of spiritual enlightenment and transformation.

Alchemy, in its essence, is the pursuit of spiritual transformation and the attainment of divine knowledge. The alchemists sought to transmute base metals into gold, but this was only a symbolic representation of their true goal: the transformation of the human soul.

In the pursuit of this goal, alchemists developed a highly symbolic language to represent the processes and stages of transformation. The alchemical symbol of the philosopher's stone, for example, represents the culmination of the alchemist's work, the attainment of spiritual enlightenment and the transmutation of the human soul.

The symbolism and philosophy of alchemy had a significant influence on esoteric traditions, including Freemasonry. Many of the symbols and concepts of alchemy can be found in Masonic ritual and symbolism, such as the concept of the "rough ashlar" representing the unrefined state of the human soul, and the "perfect ashlar" representing the ideal of spiritual transformation and enlightenment.

The use of alchemical symbolism in Freemasonry is not just limited to the Craft Lodge, but can also be found in other Masonic degrees, such as the Royal Arch and the Scottish Rite. In the Royal Arch, for example, the symbol of the blazing star represents the divine light of wisdom and knowledge, while the symbol of the triple tau represents the threefold nature of man (physical, emotional, and spiritual) and the alchemical process of transformation.

The Scottish Rite also incorporates alchemical symbolism in its degrees, with the 18th degree featuring the symbol of the pelican feeding its young with its own blood, representing self-sacrifice for the attainment of spiritual transformation.

Overall, the alchemical tradition has played a significant role in esotericism and Freemasonry, with its symbols and concepts providing a framework for the pursuit of spiritual transformation and enlightenment. The use of alchemical symbolism in Masonic ritual and symbolism serves as a reminder of the importance of this pursuit, and of the transformative power of the human spirit.

The influence of alchemy on Freemasonry goes beyond symbolism, however. The alchemical tradition also emphasized the importance of personal transformation through a process of purification and refinement. This process was seen as necessary for the attainment of spiritual enlightenment and the transmutation of the human soul.

Similarly, in Freemasonry, the initiation process is intended to be a transformative experience, in which the candidate is symbolically purified and refined in preparation for their journey towards spiritual enlightenment. The use of alchemical symbolism in Masonic ritual thus serves to reinforce the importance of this transformative process, and to encourage Masons to pursue their own personal journey towards spiritual growth and enlightenment.

Moreover, the alchemical tradition also placed a great emphasis on secrecy and the use of coded language and symbols to communicate its teachings. This emphasis on secrecy and coded language is reflected in the ritual and symbolism of Freemasonry, which also makes use of coded language and symbols to convey its teachings to initiates.

Overall, the influence of the alchemical tradition on Freemasonry can be seen in its symbolism, philosophy, and emphasis on personal transformation. By drawing upon the rich symbolism and philosophy of alchemy, Freemasonry provides a framework for its members to pursue their own personal journey towards spiritual enlightenment and the transmutation of the human soul.

In addition to its influence on Freemasonry, the alchemical tradition has also had a significant impact on Western esotericism more broadly. From the medieval period through to the Enlightenment, alchemy was seen as a key means of understanding the natural world, and was closely linked to the development of modern science.

At the same time, however, alchemy also retained a strong spiritual and philosophical dimension, and many of its practitioners saw it as a means of attaining spiritual enlightenment and the transmutation of the human soul. The alchemical tradition thus embodied a complex blend of scientific, philosophical, and spiritual elements, which had a profound influence on Western esotericism.

One of the most famous alchemical texts is the Emerald Tablet, a short cryptic text attributed to the legendary figure of Hermes Trismegistus. The Emerald Tablet is said to contain the key to the alchemical process of transmutation, and has been a source of fascination and inspiration for alchemists and esotericists for centuries.

The influence of the alchemical tradition can also be seen in the work of many other esoteric and occult figures, including Paracelsus, John Dee, and Aleister Crowley. In particular, the idea of personal transformation through a process of purification and refinement has been a central theme in much esoteric and occult literature, and can be traced back to the alchemical tradition.

Chapter 10 The Gnostic Tradition

A study of the Gnostic philosophy and its connections to esotericism and Freemasonry.

The Gnostic tradition is a philosophical and religious movement that emerged during the early Christian period, around the 2nd century CE. Gnosticism is a complex and varied system of beliefs, but at its core, it emphasizes the search for a hidden knowledge, or gnosis, that leads to spiritual enlightenment and liberation. Gnostics believed that this knowledge was not accessible through conventional means, but required a direct personal experience or revelation.

The roots of Gnosticism can be traced back to the ancient Middle East, where a number of religious and philosophical traditions emerged that emphasized the search for hidden knowledge. These included the Persian religion of Zoroastrianism, the Jewish mystical tradition of Kabbalah, and the ancient Egyptian religion of Isis and Osiris. Gnosticism also drew upon the teachings of early Christian sects such as the Ebionites and the Marcionites.

In the Gnostic worldview, the material world was seen as a flawed and imperfect creation, the result of a divine error or fall. The true spiritual realm, on the other hand, was seen as perfect and unchanging, and the goal of the Gnostic was to escape the material world and attain union with the divine.

The Gnostic tradition also placed a great deal of emphasis on the importance of individual spiritual experience and direct revelation. Gnostics believed that the search for gnosis was a personal journey that required a deep understanding of oneself and one's place in the universe. This emphasis on individualism and personal experience is a key characteristic of the esoteric traditions that followed in the centuries that followed.

Freemasonry has long been associated with the Gnostic tradition, and many of its rituals and symbols draw upon Gnostic teachings. For example, the concept of the "lost word" in Freemasonry is believed to be a reference to the Gnostic search for hidden knowledge. Similarly, the Masonic symbol of the "all-seeing eye" is thought to have its roots in the Gnostic concept of the divine spark within each individual.

The Gnostic tradition has also influenced a number of other esoteric movements, including Hermeticism, alchemy, and the occult. The mystical teachings of the Gnostics have been interpreted in a variety of ways over the centuries, and their influence can be seen in everything from the writings of William Blake to the teachings of the modern New Age movement.

Overall, the Gnostic tradition is a complex and multifaceted movement that has had a profound impact on the development of esotericism and Freemasonry. Its emphasis on individual spiritual experience and the search for hidden knowledge has inspired countless seekers throughout the centuries and continues to influence spiritual seekers today.

The Gnostic tradition has had a significant impact on esotericism and, in turn, Freemasonry. This chapter will delve deeper into the history and beliefs of the Gnostic tradition and its relevance to Freemasonry.

The term "gnostic" comes from the Greek word gnosis, meaning knowledge. Gnosticism refers to a set of religious and philosophical beliefs that emerged in the early Christian era, which emphasized the attainment of secret knowledge as the path to salvation. Gnosticism emerged as a response to the orthodox Christian teachings of the time, which emphasized faith and obedience to the Church as the means of attaining salvation.

The Gnostic tradition is characterized by a belief in the existence of a hidden and divine knowledge that can only be attained through direct personal experience. This knowledge is believed to reveal the true nature of the universe and the human soul, and to provide the means for attaining spiritual liberation and salvation.

In Gnostic belief, the material world is seen as a flawed and corrupt creation, the result of the work of an evil or ignorant deity known as the Demiurge. The Demiurge is seen as a lesser god who created the physical world and the human body, trapping the divine spark within humanity. The goal of the Gnostic is to awaken to the true nature of the self and the universe and to escape the material world and the control of the Demiurge.

The Gnostic tradition is also characterized by the use of myths and symbols to convey its teachings. These myths and symbols were often drawn from various cultural and religious traditions, including Greek, Egyptian, and Jewish traditions.

The Gnostic tradition has had a significant influence on esotericism, particularly in its emphasis on the attainment of secret knowledge and the use of symbols to convey its teachings. Many esoteric traditions, including Freemasonry, have incorporated Gnostic elements into their beliefs and practices.

In Freemasonry, the Gnostic tradition is reflected in its emphasis on the attainment of knowledge through study and contemplation. Masonic symbolism, such as the blazing star, the all-seeing eye, and the ladder of ascent, is also believed to have Gnostic roots. The search for spiritual enlightenment and the liberation of the soul from the material world are key themes in both the Gnostic tradition and Freemasonry.

Chapter 11 The Chakra System

An overview of the chakra system and its significance in esoteric traditions and Freemasonry.

The chakra system is an ancient concept found in various esoteric traditions, including Hinduism, Buddhism, and Taoism. The word "chakra" comes from the Sanskrit language, meaning "wheel" or "disk," and refers to the spinning energy centers that are believed to exist within the subtle body. The chakras are seen as centers of spiritual power that correspond to different physical, emotional, and mental functions.

There are seven major chakras in the human body, each located in a specific area and associated with a particular color, element, and sound. These chakras are arranged along the spinal cord and are often represented as lotus flowers with a varying number of petals.

In esoteric traditions, the chakras are believed to be important for achieving spiritual enlightenment and developing psychic abilities. In Freemasonry, the chakras are not explicitly mentioned, but some of the practices and rituals involve the cultivation of spiritual energy, which can be seen as a similar concept.

The first chakra, located at the base of the spine, is the root chakra. It is associated with the element of earth, the color red, and the sound "Lam." This chakra is related to our sense of security, stability, and survival instincts. In esoteric traditions, it is believed that the root chakra must be balanced and strong before one can move on to the higher chakras.

The second chakra, located in the lower abdomen, is the sacral chakra. It is associated with the element of water, the color orange, and the sound "Vam." This chakra is related to our sexuality, creativity, and emotional expression.

The third chakra, located in the solar plexus, is the solar plexus chakra. It is associated with the element of fire, the color yellow, and the sound "Ram." This chakra is related to our personal power, self-confidence, and willpower.

The fourth chakra, located in the center of the chest, is the heart chakra. It is associated with the element of air, the color green, and the sound "Yam." This chakra is related to our ability to love, forgive, and connect with others.

The fifth chakra, located in the throat, is the throat chakra. It is associated with the element of ether or space, the color blue, and the sound "Ham." This chakra is related to our ability to communicate effectively and express ourselves creatively.

The sixth chakra, located in the center of the forehead, is the third eye chakra. It is associated with the element of light, the color indigo, and the sound "Om." This chakra is related to our intuition, psychic abilities, and spiritual insight.

The seventh chakra, located at the crown of the head, is the crown chakra. It is associated with the element of consciousness, the color violet, and the sound "Aum." This chakra is related to our connection to the divine and our spiritual enlightenment.

In esoteric traditions, it is believed that by working with the chakras, one can achieve greater physical health, emotional balance, and spiritual enlightenment. In Freemasonry, some of the practices and rituals involve the cultivation of spiritual energy, which can be seen as a similar concept. However, the chakra system is not explicitly mentioned in Freemasonry, and it is up to the individual Mason to explore and incorporate these concepts into their personal spiritual practice.

Chapter 12 The Astral Plane

An examination of the concept of the astral plane and its role in esotericism and Freemasonry.

The astral plane is a concept that has been present in esoteric traditions for centuries. It is believed to be a non-physical realm of existence that is said to be inhabited by spirits, entities, and even the souls of the deceased. The astral plane is also said to be the place where many esoteric practices such as astral projection and dream work take place.

In esotericism, the astral plane is seen as a realm that is closely linked to the physical world. It is believed that everything that exists in the physical world has a corresponding form on the astral plane. This means that the astral plane is seen as a reflection of the physical world, but in a non-physical form.

The astral plane is often described as having multiple levels or layers, with each level being inhabited by different types of entities or spirits. Some esoteric traditions believe that the astral plane can be divided into seven levels, each of which corresponds to one of the seven chakras. This idea is similar to the concept of the seven heavens that is present in many religions.

The astral plane is also believed to be a place where individuals can go to learn and develop spiritually. In esotericism, it is said that individuals can access the astral plane through various spiritual practices such as meditation, astral projection, and lucid dreaming. By doing so, individuals can connect with their higher selves, access higher levels of consciousness, and gain spiritual insights and knowledge.

In Freemasonry, the concept of the astral plane is also present. It is believed that the astral plane can be accessed through certain Masonic practices and rituals, and that it is a place where Masons can connect with the spiritual realm and gain knowledge and insights that can help them in their Masonic journey.

Overall, the concept of the astral plane is a complex and fascinating topic that has played an important role in esotericism and Freemasonry for centuries. It is a realm that is believed to be closely linked to the physical world, and one that individuals can access through various spiritual practices in order to gain spiritual insights and knowledge.

The astral plane is said to be a realm of existence that is beyond the physical realm, yet still intimately connected to it. It is believed by some esoteric traditions to be a plane of existence that can be accessed through meditation, astral projection, and other spiritual practices. In Freemasonry, the concept of the astral plane is often referred to as the "inner plane," and is considered to be a realm of spiritual growth and transformation.

The origins of the concept of the astral plane can be traced back to ancient Eastern philosophies, such as Hinduism and Buddhism. These traditions believed in the existence of a subtle body, composed of energy, that could travel beyond the physical body into other realms of existence. The concept of the astral plane was further developed in the West by the Theosophical Society, a spiritual organization that emerged in the late 19th century and had a significant influence on esotericism and Freemasonry.

According to Theosophy, the astral plane is one of seven planes of existence, with the physical plane being the lowest and the spiritual plane being the highest. The astral plane is said to be a realm of thought and emotion, where individuals can experience various states of consciousness and interact with beings that exist on that plane. It is believed that the astral plane is populated by beings such as spirits, angels, and demons, as well as by the astral bodies of individuals who have died.

In Freemasonry, the concept of the astral plane is closely connected to the idea of inner transformation and spiritual growth. It is believed that by accessing the inner plane through meditation and other spiritual practices, individuals can gain insight into their true nature and the nature of the universe. Freemasonry encourages its members to seek knowledge and understanding of the inner plane, as it is believed to be a key component of the Masonic journey.

The symbolism of the astral plane is often represented by the image of a ladder or staircase, with each step representing a higher level of consciousness or spiritual awareness. In Masonic ritual, the ladder symbolizes the journey of the individual from darkness to light, from ignorance to knowledge, and from mortality to immortality. The ladder is also a symbol of the individual's ascent to the inner plane, where they can access higher levels of consciousness and spiritual understanding.

Chapter 13 The Role of Meditation

A discussion of the importance of meditation in esoteric traditions and how it is used in Freemasonry.

Meditation is a practice that has been used for thousands of years in various spiritual and esoteric traditions around the world. It involves training the mind to focus and become aware of the present moment, ultimately leading to a state of inner peace and stillness. In esotericism and Freemasonry, meditation is seen as a powerful tool for spiritual development and self-discovery.

Origins of Meditation

The origins of meditation can be traced back to ancient India, where it was used as a tool for spiritual development and enlightenment. The earliest written record of meditation comes from the Hindu Vedas, which date back to around 1500 BCE. The practice of meditation was later adopted by other spiritual traditions, including Buddhism, Taoism, and Sufism.

Meditation in Esotericism

In esoteric traditions, meditation is seen as a way to connect with the divine and access higher levels of consciousness. It is often used as a tool for spiritual development and self-discovery, helping individuals to better understand themselves and their place in the universe. Through regular meditation practice, one can cultivate a deeper sense of inner peace, clarity, and intuition.

Meditation is also seen as a way to develop psychic abilities and connect with the astral plane. In some esoteric traditions, meditation is used to access higher levels of consciousness and commune with spiritual beings or entities.

Meditation in Freemasonry

In Freemasonry, meditation is seen as a way to connect with the divine and access higher levels of consciousness. It is often used as a tool for spiritual development and self-discovery, helping Masons to better understand themselves and their place in the universe.

Meditation is also used in Masonic ritual, particularly during the opening and closing ceremonies of lodges. These meditative practices help Masons to enter a state of inner calm and focus, enabling them to better connect with the symbolism and teachings of the Craft.

Types of Meditation

There are many different types of meditation, each with its own unique focus and approach. Some of the most common types of meditation include:

1. Mindfulness meditation: This involves focusing on the present moment and observing one's thoughts and feelings without judgment.
2. Transcendental meditation: This involves using a mantra or phrase to focus the mind and achieve a state of deep relaxation.
3. Loving-kindness meditation: This involves cultivating feelings of love, kindness, and compassion towards oneself and others.
4. Chakra meditation: This involves focusing on the energy centers in the body known as chakras, with the goal of balancing and harmonizing the flow of energy.

Benefits of Meditation

Regular meditation practice has been shown to have a wide range of benefits, including:

1. Reduced stress and anxiety
2. Improved focus and concentration
3. Increased self-awareness
4. Improved emotional regulation
5. Increased feelings of inner peace and calm
6. Improved physical health, including lower blood pressure and reduced inflammation.

Chapter 14 The Great Work

An exploration of the concept of the Great Work and its significance in esotericism and Freemasonry.

The Great Work is a central concept in esoteric traditions and Freemasonry. It refers to the pursuit of spiritual transformation, enlightenment, and the attainment of a higher level of consciousness. In this chapter, we will explore the origins of the Great Work, its meaning, and its role in esotericism and Freemasonry.

The origins of the Great Work can be traced back to the alchemical tradition, where it referred to the pursuit of the philosopher's stone, a legendary substance believed to have the power to transform base metals into gold and to grant immortality. In the context of esotericism and Freemasonry, the Great Work is understood as a spiritual and mystical journey that involves the transformation of the individual's inner being.

The Great Work is often associated with the pursuit of knowledge, self-discovery, and spiritual growth. It involves a process of inner transformation that leads to a deeper understanding of the self and the universe. This process requires the cultivation of virtues such as patience, perseverance, and humility, as well as the development of spiritual practices such as meditation and prayer.

In the context of Freemasonry, the Great Work is closely tied to the concept of building. Just as the medieval stonemasons built cathedrals and other structures, the Masonic initiate is called to build the temple of the self. This involves the purification of the mind, body, and soul, as well as the cultivation of virtues and the practice of charity.

The Great Work is a never-ending process, as the pursuit of spiritual growth and enlightenment is a lifelong journey. However, it is believed that through the practice of spiritual disciplines and the cultivation of virtue, the individual can make progress towards the ultimate goal of the Great Work.

One of the key symbols of the Great Work is the ouroboros, an ancient symbol depicting a serpent or dragon eating its own tail. The ouroboros represents the cyclical nature of life, death, and rebirth, and the idea that the end of one cycle is the beginning of another. It also represents the idea of unity and wholeness, as the serpent symbolizes the individual's journey towards integration and balance.

Chapter 15 The Future of Esotericism

A look at the current state of esotericism and its potential future, including its relationship to Freemasonry and its role in contemporary culture.

Esotericism has a rich and complex history that spans thousands of years and encompasses a wide range of traditions and practices. As we move further into the 21st century, the study and practice of esotericism continues to evolve and change. In this chapter, we will examine the current state of esotericism and its potential future, including its relationship to Freemasonry and its role in contemporary culture.

The Current State of Esotericism

Esotericism has experienced a resurgence in recent years, with many people turning to ancient traditions and spiritual practices in search of meaning and purpose in their lives. This renewed interest in esotericism has led to a proliferation of books, classes, and workshops on subjects such as astrology, tarot, and meditation.

One of the reasons for this renewed interest in esotericism is the growing awareness of the limitations of mainstream religion and science. Many people find that these institutions do not fully address their spiritual or intellectual needs, and they are turning to esotericism as a way to explore the mysteries of the universe and their place in it.

Esotericism has also been embraced by popular culture, with references to occult symbols and practices appearing in movies, music, and television shows. This mainstream exposure has helped to bring esotericism to a wider audience and has sparked an interest in the subject among a new generation of seekers.

The Future of Esotericism

As we move into the future, it is likely that esotericism will continue to evolve and change. One of the most significant trends in contemporary esotericism is the integration of technology and spirituality. Many esoteric practitioners are exploring the use of virtual reality and other technologies to create immersive spiritual experiences.

Another trend is the development of new esoteric practices that draw on ancient traditions while incorporating modern insights and techniques. For example, many practitioners are combining traditional astrology with modern psychology to create a more holistic approach to understanding the self.

Esotericism is also becoming more accessible to a wider audience, with online classes, workshops, and communities making it easier than ever to learn about and practice esoteric traditions. This increased accessibility is likely to continue, with esotericism becoming more mainstream and less stigmatized.

The Role of Freemasonry in the Future of Esotericism

Freemasonry has long been associated with esotericism, and its role in the future of esotericism is likely to be significant. Freemasonry provides a community of like-minded individuals who are interested in exploring the mysteries of the universe and their place in it.

Freemasonry also provides a framework for the study and practice of esotericism, with its degrees and initiations providing a structured path for spiritual development. As more people turn to esotericism, Freemasonry is likely to continue to attract new members and provide a community for those seeking spiritual growth and knowledge.